WASHINGTON NATIONALS
ALL-TIME GREATS

BY BRENDAN FLYNN

Copyright © 2021 by Press Room Editions. All rights reserved. No part of this book may be used or reproduced in any manner whatsoever, including internet usage, without written permission from the copyright owner, except in the case of brief quotations embodied in critical articles and reviews.

Book design by Jake Slavik
Cover design by Jake Slavik

Photographs ©: Kyodo/AP Images, cover (top), 1 (top); Tom DiPace/AP Images, cover (bottom), 1 (bottom), 9, 18; Focus on Sport/Getty Images, 4; Bill Grimshaw/AP Images, 6; Andrew D. Bernstein/Getty Images Sport/Getty Images, 10; David Durochik/AP Images, 12; Mike Poche/AP Images, 13; Matt York/AP Images, 15; Winslow Townson/AP Images, 16; Nick Wass/AP Images, 19; Andrew Harnik/AP Images, 20; Red Line Editorial, 22

Press Box Books, an imprint of Press Room Editions.

ISBN
978-1-63494-296-6 (library bound)
978-1-63494-314-7 (paperback)
978-1-63494-350-5 (epub)
978-1-63494-332-1 (hosted ebook)

Library of Congress Control Number: 2020913873

Distributed by North Star Editions, Inc.
2297 Waters Drive
Mendota Heights, MN 55120
www.northstareditions.com

Printed in the United States of America
012021

ABOUT THE AUTHOR

Brendan Flynn is a San Francisco resident and an author of numerous children's books. In addition to writing about sports, Flynn also enjoys competing in triathlons, Scrabble tournaments, and chili cook-offs.

TABLE OF CONTENTS

STAUB
10

CHAPTER 1
EARLY EXPOS

Major League Baseball went international on April 14, 1969. That was the day of the first home game of the Montreal Expos. They were one of two National League (NL) expansion teams that year.

Hitting third and playing right field on Opening Day was **Rusty Staub**. Staub brought a veteran presence to the brand-new Expos. He batted .302 and was the team's first All-Star. His power hitting and friendly nature made him a fan favorite in Montreal.

CARTER
8

Steve Rogers was the Expos' first true staff ace. Rogers was a five-time All-Star and led the league in earned run average (ERA) in 1982. His 158 wins are the most in Expos history.

The Expos built themselves into a playoff contender throughout the 1970s. Catcher **Gary Carter** was a big boost to the lineup. An enthusiastic and popular player, Carter contributed with

RETIRED NUMBERS

All of the Expos' retired numbers come from the 1980s teams. They retired No. 10 for both Dawson and Staub, No. 8 for Gary Carter, and No. 30 for Tim Raines. When the team moved in 2005 to become the Washington Nationals, the Nationals made all these numbers available. A banner honoring these players now hangs at the home of the Montreal Canadiens hockey team.

his bat and his glove. He hit two homers and drove in six runs to help the Expos win their first playoff series in 1981.

The man who carried that 1981 team was outfielder **Andre Dawson**. He finished second in NL Most Valuable Player (MVP) voting that year. Dawson was often an MVP-caliber player in his 11 seasons in Montreal. He hit for power and had a devastating throwing arm from the outfield. NL base runners learned quickly that nobody ran on "The Hawk."

Speedster **Tim Raines** was a seven-time All-Star in left field for Montreal. He led the NL in stolen bases each year from 1981 to 1984. Often hitting leadoff, Raines set the table for the Expos lineup. He stole more bases and scored more runs than anyone else in team history.

Third baseman **Tim Wallach** was a thrill to watch in the field and at the plate. Wallach won three Gold Gloves for defense and two Silver Sluggers for hitting. He also was a five-time All-Star. Even though the Expos didn't do much winning in the 1980s, these players made the team exciting to watch.

STAT SPOTLIGHT

MOST CAREER STOLEN BASES
FRANCHISE RECORD
Tim Raines: 635

WALKER
33

CHAPTER 2
DYNASTY DISRUPTED

In 1991, the Expos went 71–90, finishing dead last in the NL East. But the team also featured a core of young players that would soon make them a World Series contender. As a Canadian, right fielder **Larry Walker** was an instant fan favorite. His all-around ability at the plate and in the field made him a star.

Speedy center fielder **Marquis Grissom** made his debut in 1989, the same year as Walker. He led the league in stolen bases in 1991 and 1992. He was an All-Star in 1993, when the Expos won 94 games and finished second in their division.

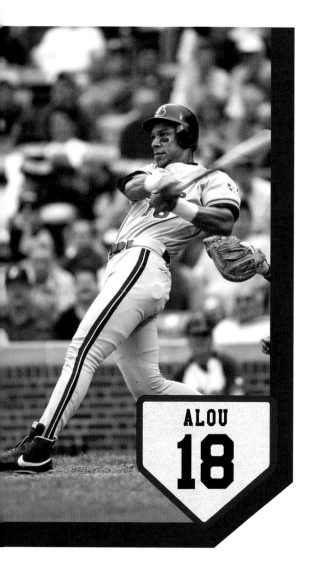

ALOU
18

The Expos got a big boost in 1990, when they traded for outfielder **Moises Alou**. Alou's father, Felipe, became Expos manager in 1992. Injuries slowed Moises Alou's development. But by 1994, he was hitting .339 as the Expos surged to the top of the standings.

Pedro Martinez came to Montreal in a trade just after the 1993 season. Previously a reliever, the Expos developed him into a dominant starter.

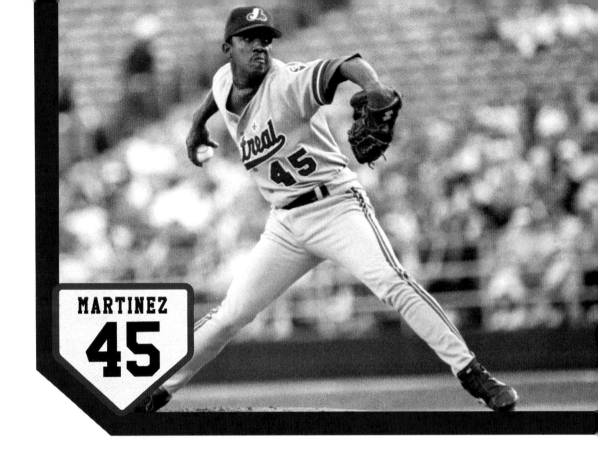

MARTINEZ
45

The young right-hander was second on the team in wins in 1994. In 1997, he won the first Cy Young Award in Expos history.

STAT SPOTLIGHT

MOST MANAGER WINS
FRANCHISE RECORD

Felipe Alou: 691

The exciting Expos had put it all together in 1994. Their young, talented core had put up the best record in baseball by August. But a players' strike ended the season early and the playoffs were canceled. The Expos never had such a great team again.

Vladimir Guerrero added some excitement to the team's final years in Montreal. The right fielder hit for both power and average. He was known as a "bad ball" hitter, able to

MISSED OPPORTUNITY

On the day a players' strike ended the 1994 MLB season, the Expos had a record of 74–40. They led their division by six games. They were third in the NL in runs scored and first in ERA. They were expected to contend for the World Series title. Instead, the Expos never got that chance. In 1995, they went 66–78 and finished last in their division.

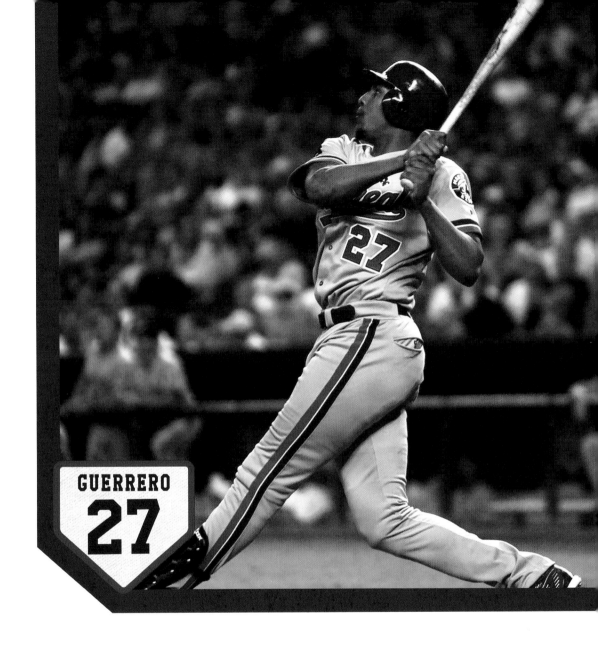

GUERRERO
27

make contact wherever the ball was pitched.
Guerrero left the Expos in 2004, their final year
in Montreal.

ZIMMERMAN
11

CHAPTER 3
CAPITAL HEROES

By 2003, the Expos were a mess. They had an aging stadium and poor attendance. They were losing money, and MLB had to take over the team's daily operations. After the 2004 season, MLB moved them to Washington, DC, where they became the Nationals.

The first-ever Nationals draft pick was **Ryan Zimmerman**. The young infielder, who grew up nearby in Virginia, sailed through the minor leagues and made his MLB debut in September 2005. Zimmerman proved to be a reliable hitter with power for the next 15 years. He hit more career home runs than any Expo or National.

HARPER
34

The Nationals did not win a lot in their early years. They hoped **Bryce Harper** would help change that. The first overall pick in the 2010 MLB Draft, Harper made his debut in 2012. The right fielder won the NL Rookie of the Year Award and led the Nats to the playoffs. He was the NL MVP in 2015 when he led the league in home runs, making him one of baseball's biggest stars.

Like Harper, pitcher **Stephen Strasburg** came into MLB with big expectations. Strasburg lived up to them, becoming the Nationals' ace. He was joined in the rotation in 2015 by **Max Scherzer**. The veteran right-hander won the NL Cy Young Award in 2016 and 2017. The Nationals were building an impressive staff.

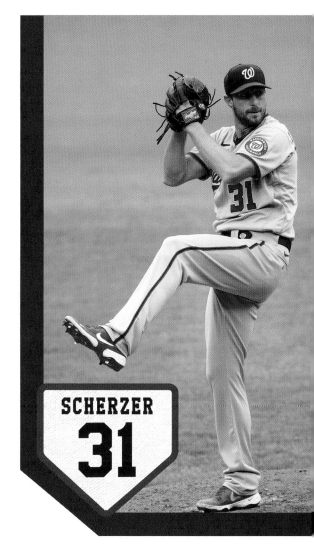

SCHERZER
31

SOTO
22

Washington's World Series dreams took a hit when Harper signed with the Philadelphia Phillies in 2019. Fortunately, the team had a new superstar-in-waiting. **Juan Soto** was just 20 years old in 2019 when he hit 34 home runs and drove in 110 runs. The outfielder's

CLUTCH SLUGGER

Anthony Rendon was another key member of the Nationals' World Series team. Rendon led the majors with 126 runs batted in that year. He drove in eight more in the World Series to lead the team.

strong play helped the Nationals win the NL pennant. He then hit .333 with three home runs in the first World Series appearance in franchise history.

But Soto was not the series MVP. That award went to Strasburg, who started and won two games as the Nationals beat the Houston Astros. It took 50 years and two countries. But they finally won it all.

STAT SPOTLIGHT

MOST CAREER HOME RUNS
FRANCHISE RECORD
Ryan Zimmerman: 270

TIMELINE

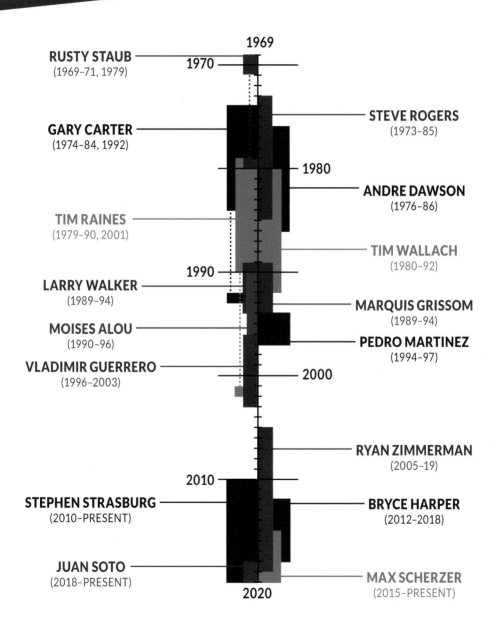

1969

RUSTY STAUB
(1969–71, 1979)

1970

STEVE ROGERS
(1973–85)

GARY CARTER
(1974–84, 1992)

1980

ANDRE DAWSON
(1976–86)

TIM RAINES
(1979–90, 2001)

TIM WALLACH
(1980–92)

1990

LARRY WALKER
(1989–94)

MARQUIS GRISSOM
(1989–94)

MOISES ALOU
(1990–96)

PEDRO MARTINEZ
(1994–97)

VLADIMIR GUERRERO
(1996–2003)

2000

RYAN ZIMMERMAN
(2005–19)

2010

STEPHEN STRASBURG
(2010–PRESENT)

BRYCE HARPER
(2012–2018)

JUAN SOTO
(2018–PRESENT)

MAX SCHERZER
(2015–PRESENT)

2020

WASHINGTON NATIONALS

Formerly: Montreal Expos (1969–2004)

World Series titles: 1 (2019)*

Key managers:

Felipe Alou (1992–2001)

691–717 (.491)

Dave Martinez (2018–present)

201–183 (.523), 1 World Series title

Gene Mauch (1969–75)

499–627 (.443)

Buck Rodgers (1985–91)

520–499 (.510)

MORE INFORMATION

To learn more about the Washington Nationals, go to **pressboxbooks.com/AllAccess**.

These links are routinely monitored and updated to provide the most current information available.

*1903 through 2019

GLOSSARY

ace
A team's best starting pitcher.

Cy Young Award
An award given every year to the best pitcher in the American League and National League.

earned run average (ERA)
A statistic that measures the average number of earned runs that a pitcher gives up per nine innings.

Gold Glove
An award given every year to the top fielder in the league at each position.

minor leagues
A lower level of baseball where players work on improving their skills before they reach the major leagues.

Silver Slugger
An award given every year to the league's best hitter at each position.

INDEX